Copyright @LindsayDuncan
All rights reserved. No part of this book may be reproduced in any form without permission from the author.

Dedication

This book is dedicated to all the children.

Cyclone Annie

Written by Lindsay Duncan

Illustrated by Sangi Parvin

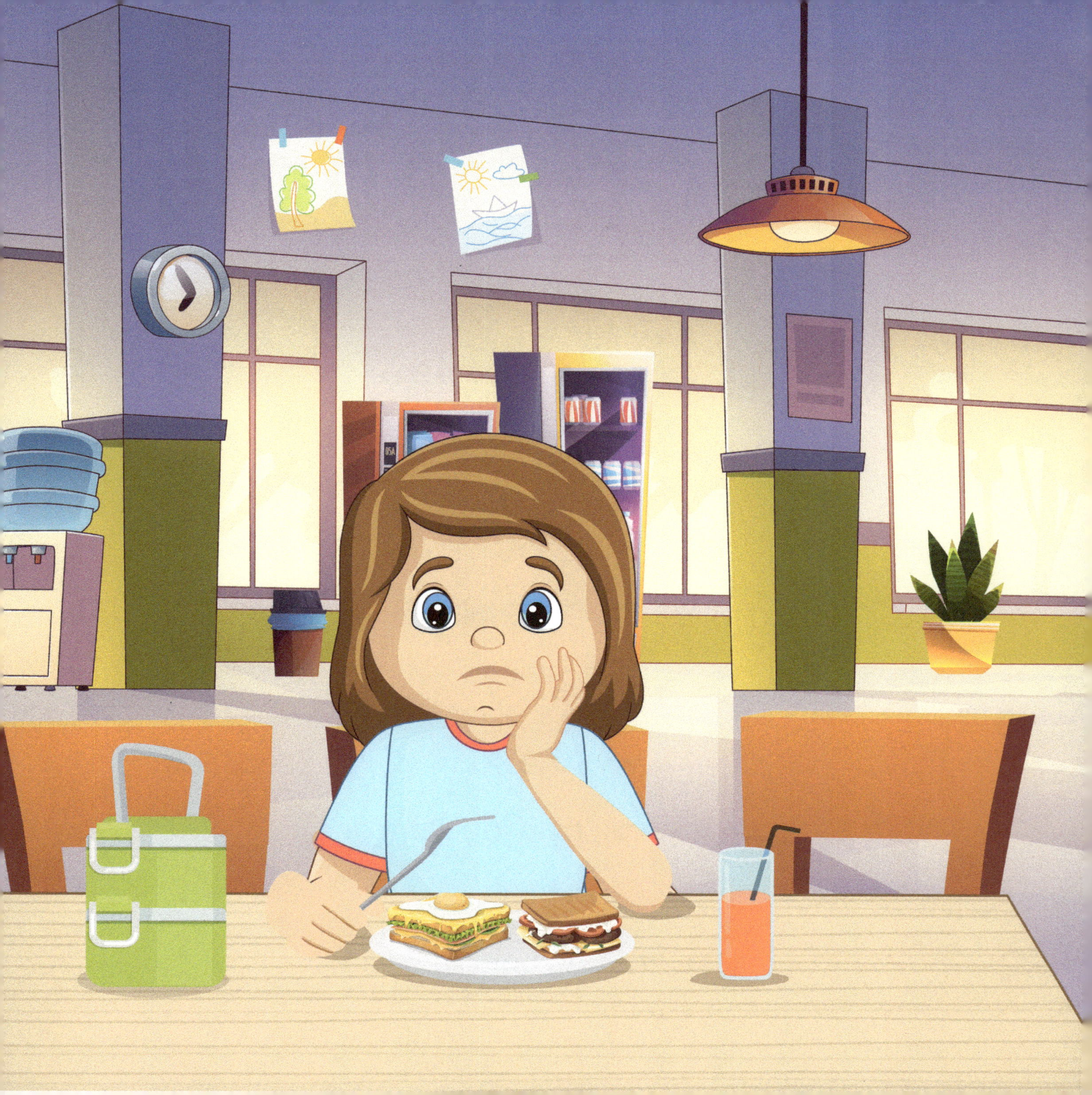

Cyclone Annie is a nice girl.
But at school, she doesn't feel she fits.
The kids are sometimes mean to her.
At lunch in a chair, all alone, she sits.

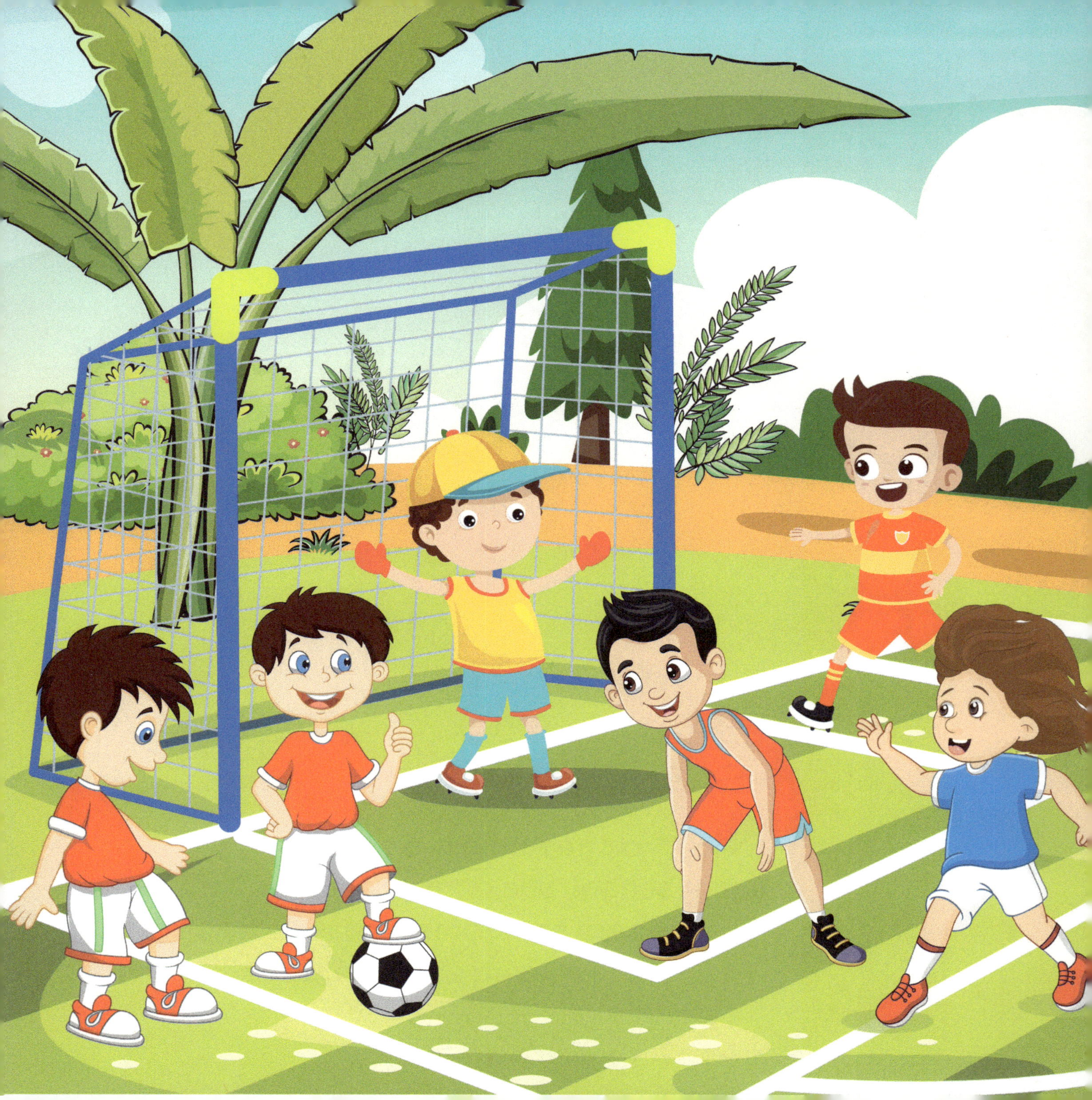

One day, she tried again.
She asked them nicely, "Can I play?
I'm good at this football game."
But they all looked the other way.

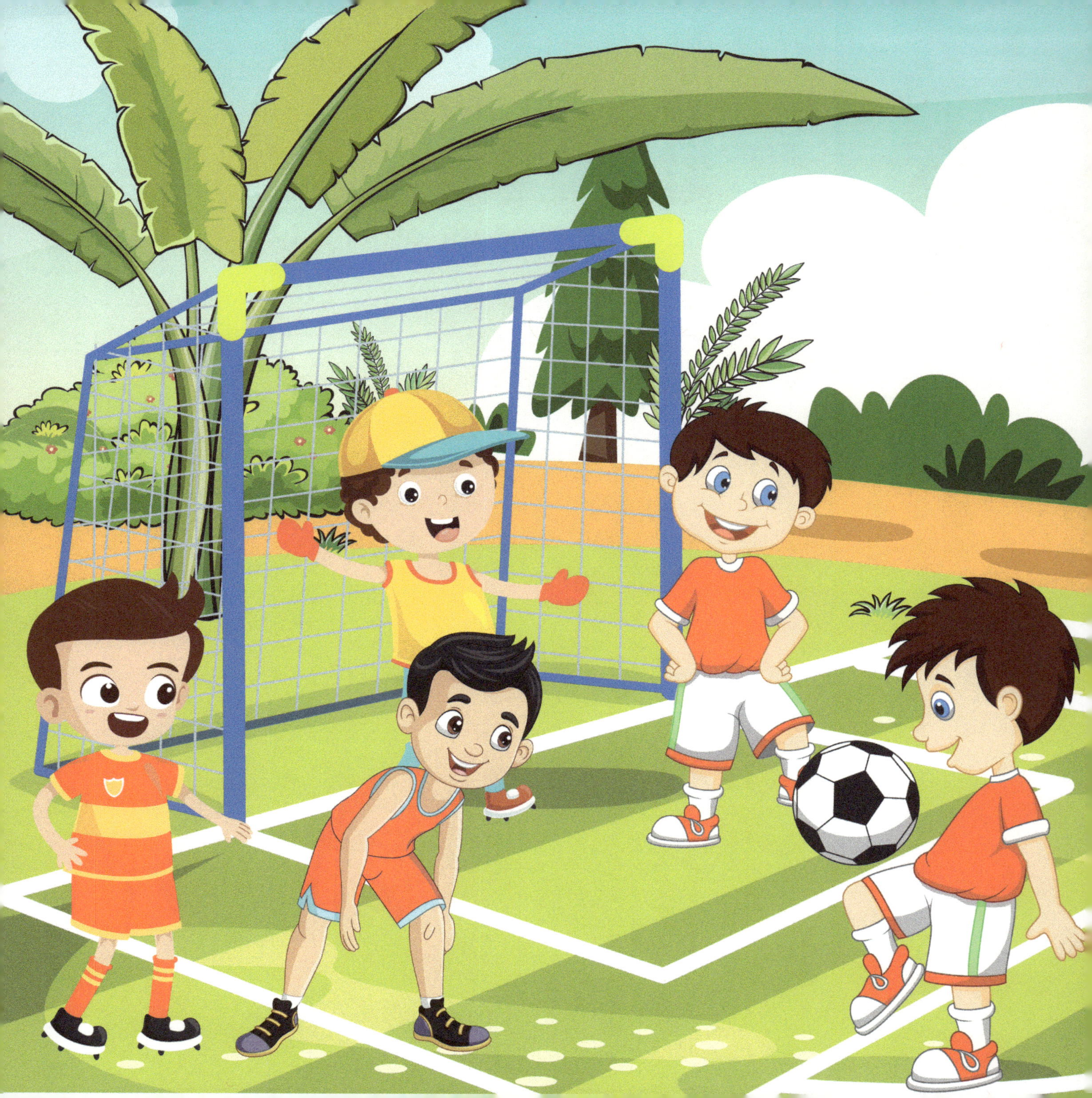

"No! Cyclone Annie.
On this side, you don't belong.
You cannot play with us.
Your wind is just too strong."

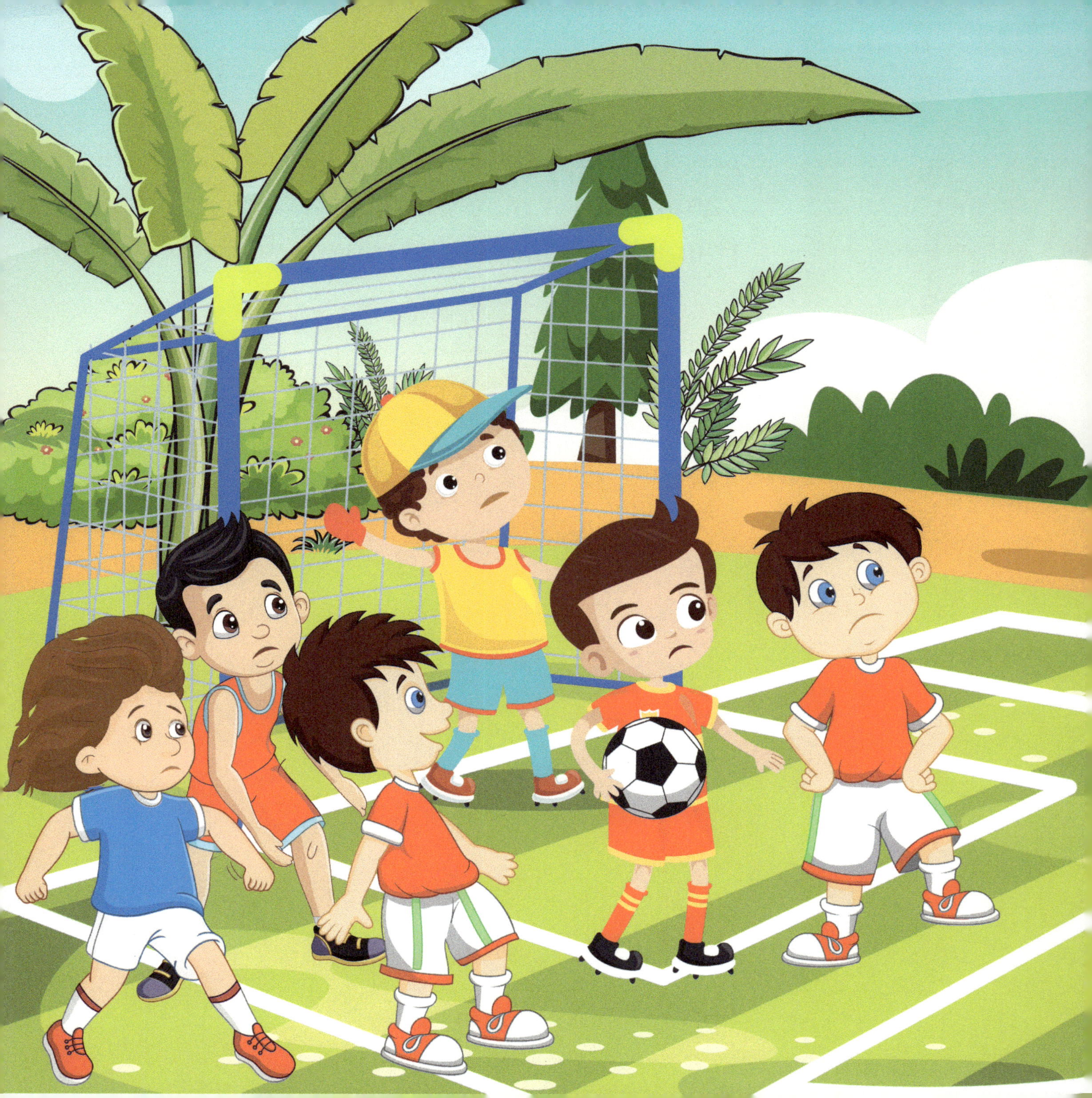

She huffed and puffed,
As she swirled herself around.
With every huff and puff,
Her anger made a sound.

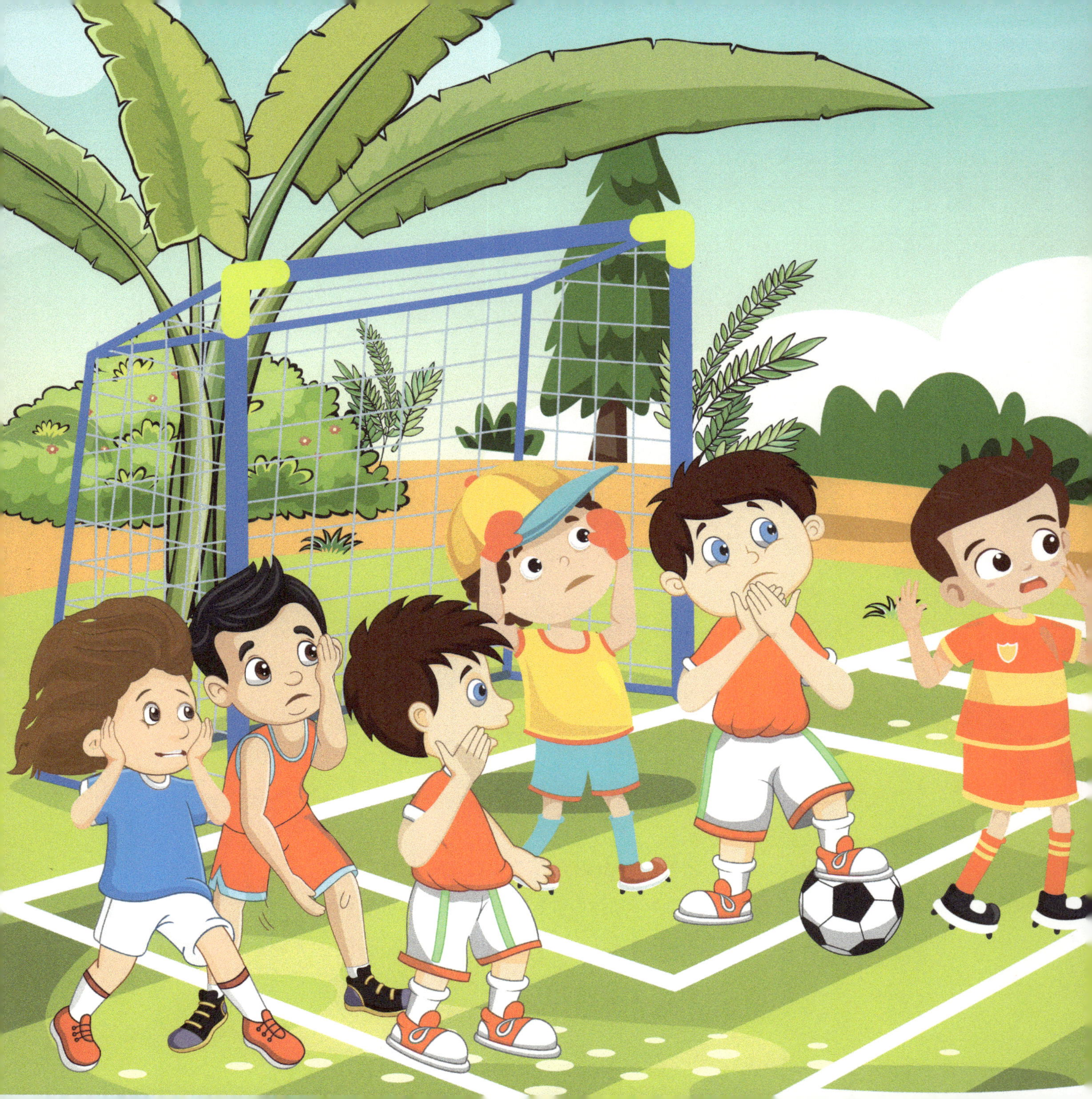

Her cyclone grew stronger,
As it moved across the ground.
Her wind legs had gotten longer,
Upset that nobody wanted her around.

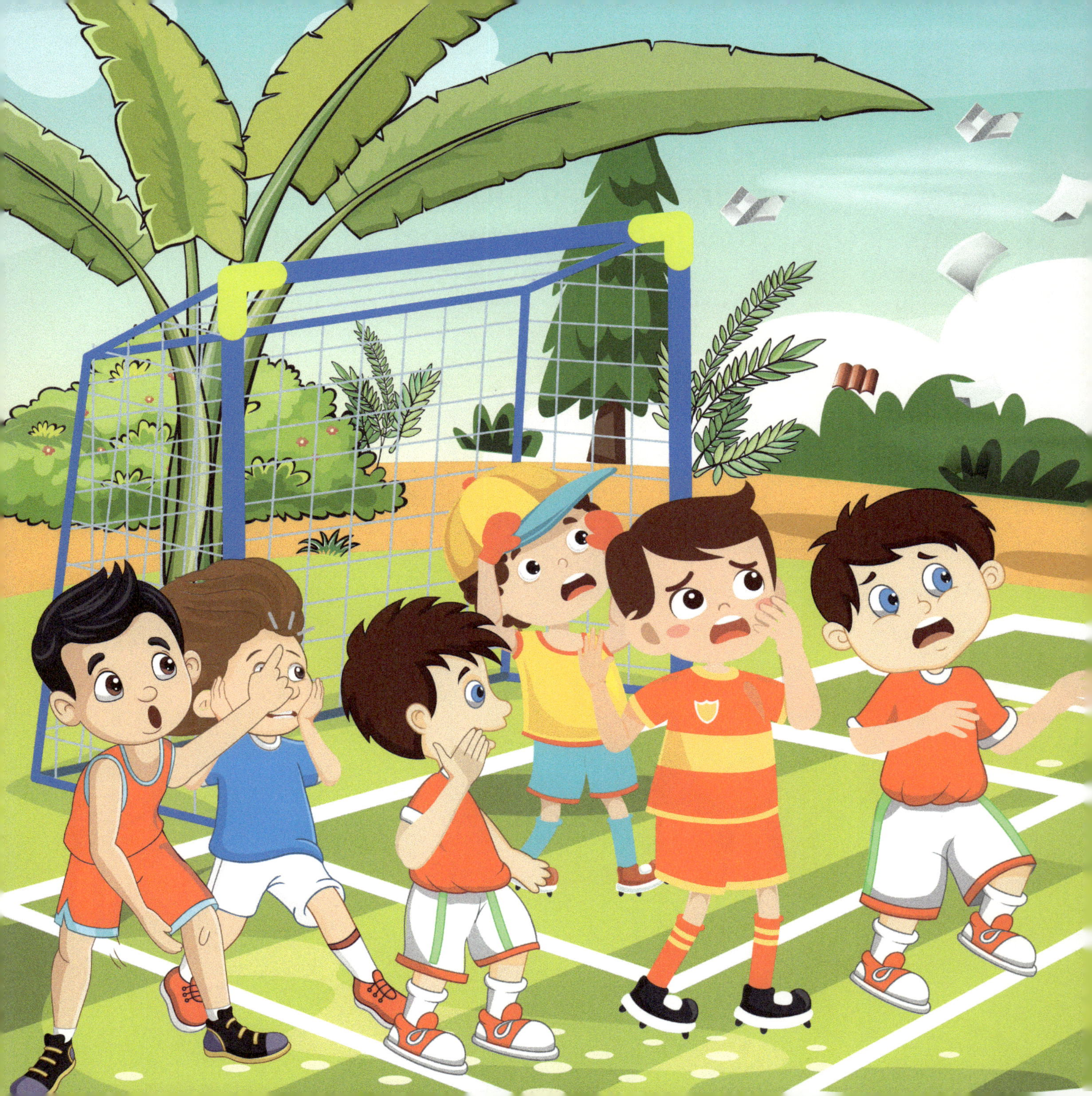

She swirled across the football field.
And blew the ball away.
That will teach them, she thought.
They should have let me play!

She saw a girl in the distance,
And moved along towards the slide.
She hovered around the girl,
But the girl soon ran inside.

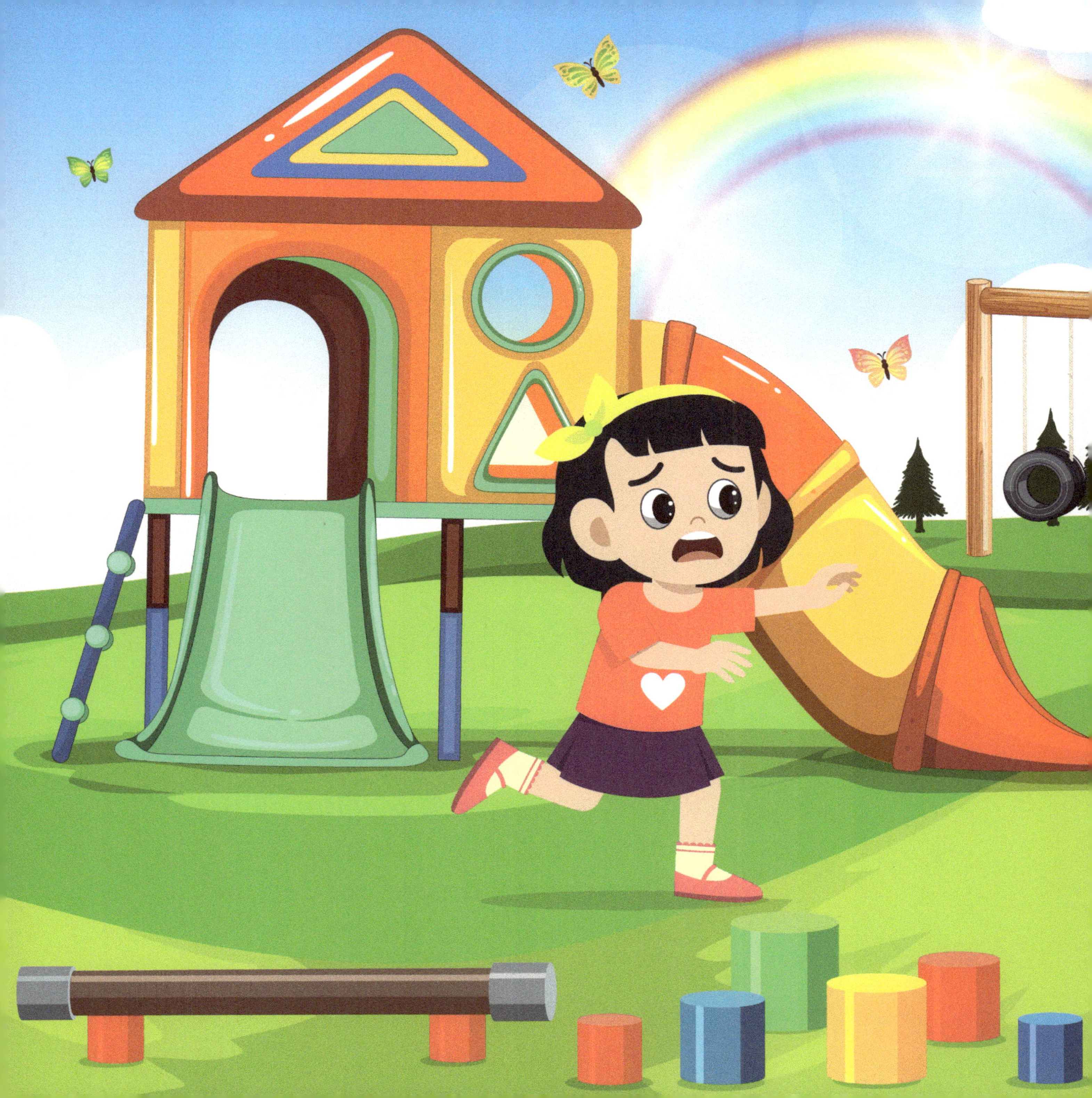

"Stop, Cyclone Annie!" the teacher said.
"Come tell me what is wrong.
For when you are so angry,
Your cyclone is strong."

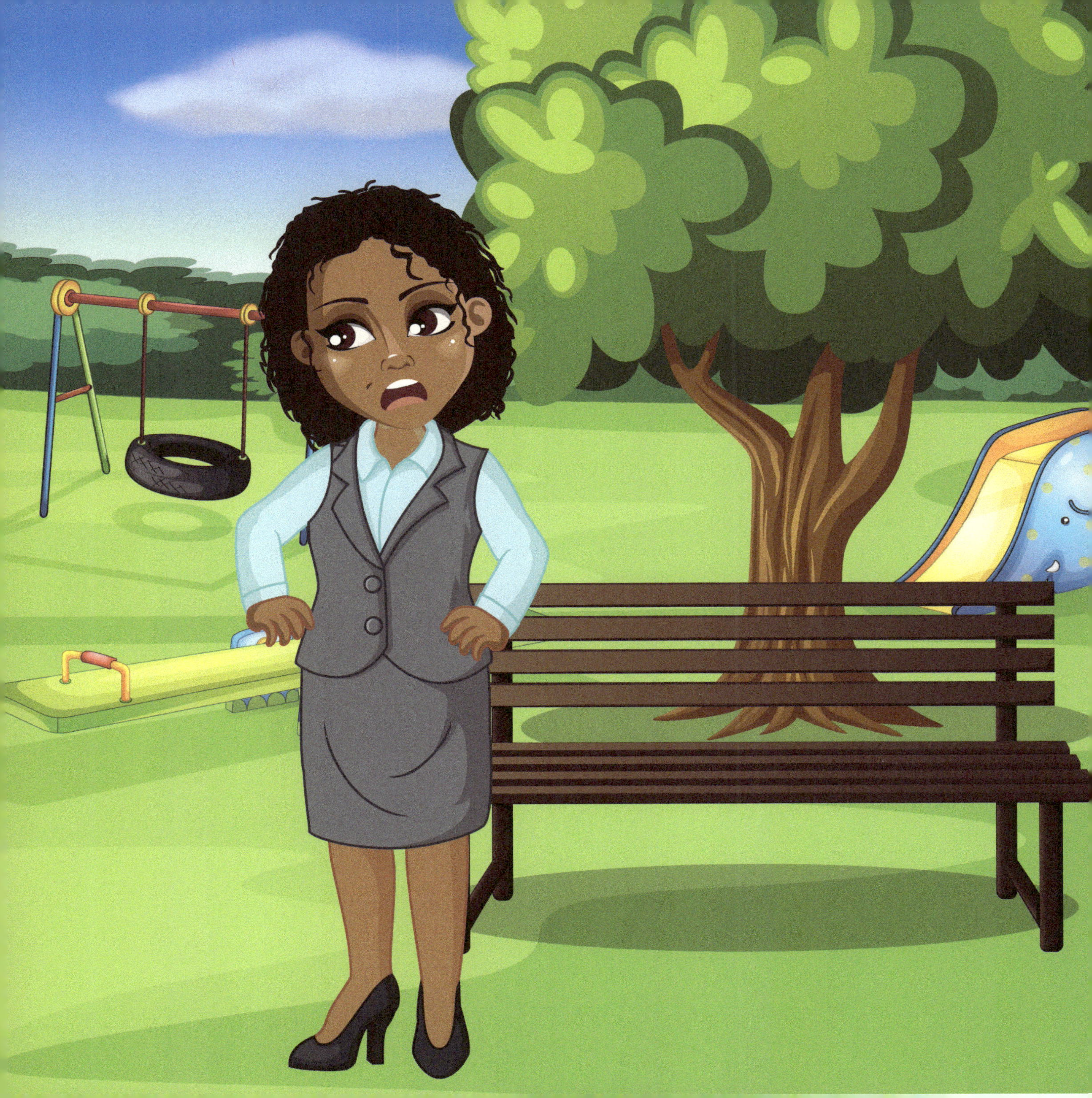

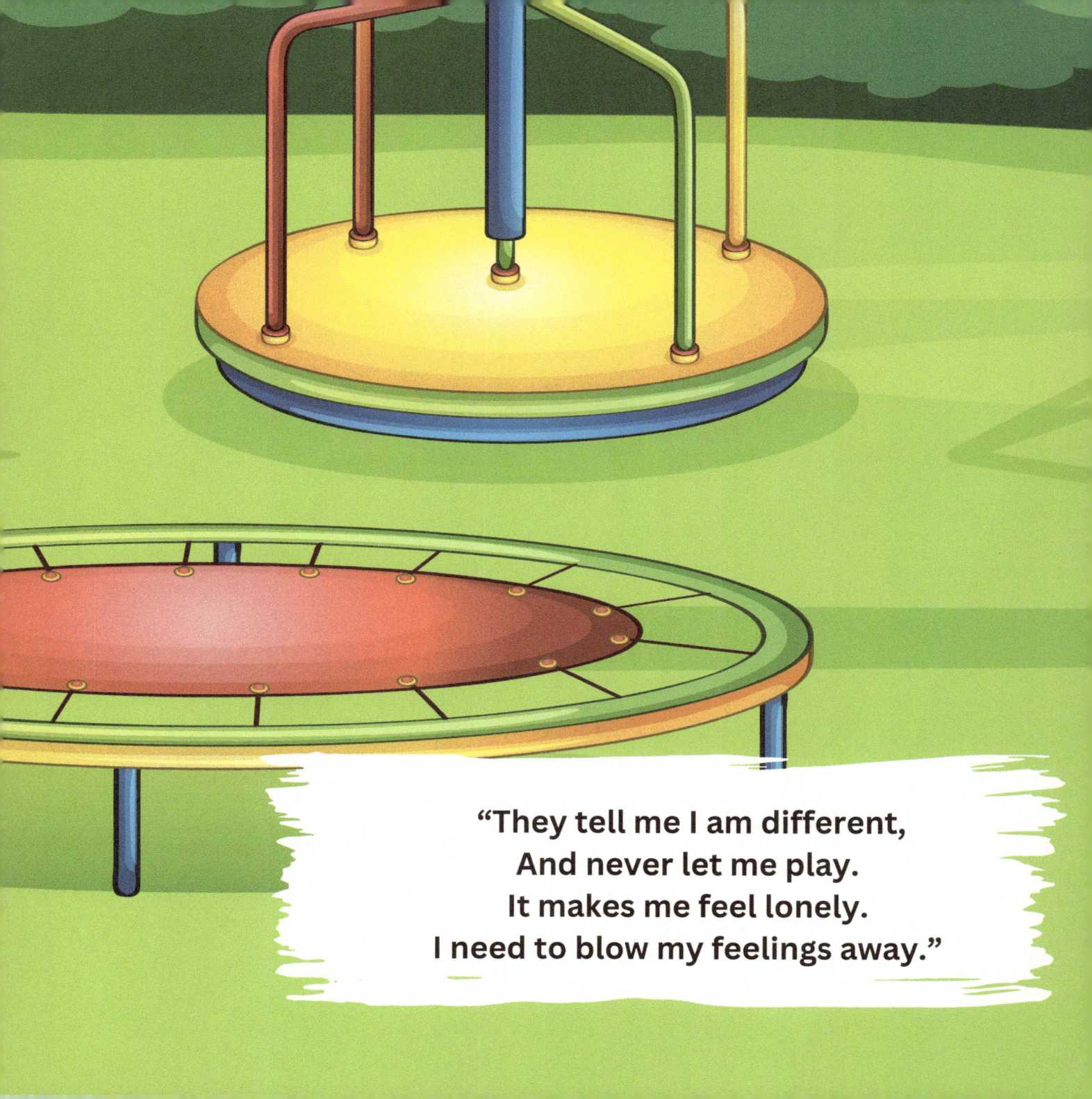

"They tell me I am different,
And never let me play.
It makes me feel lonely.
I need to blow my feelings away."

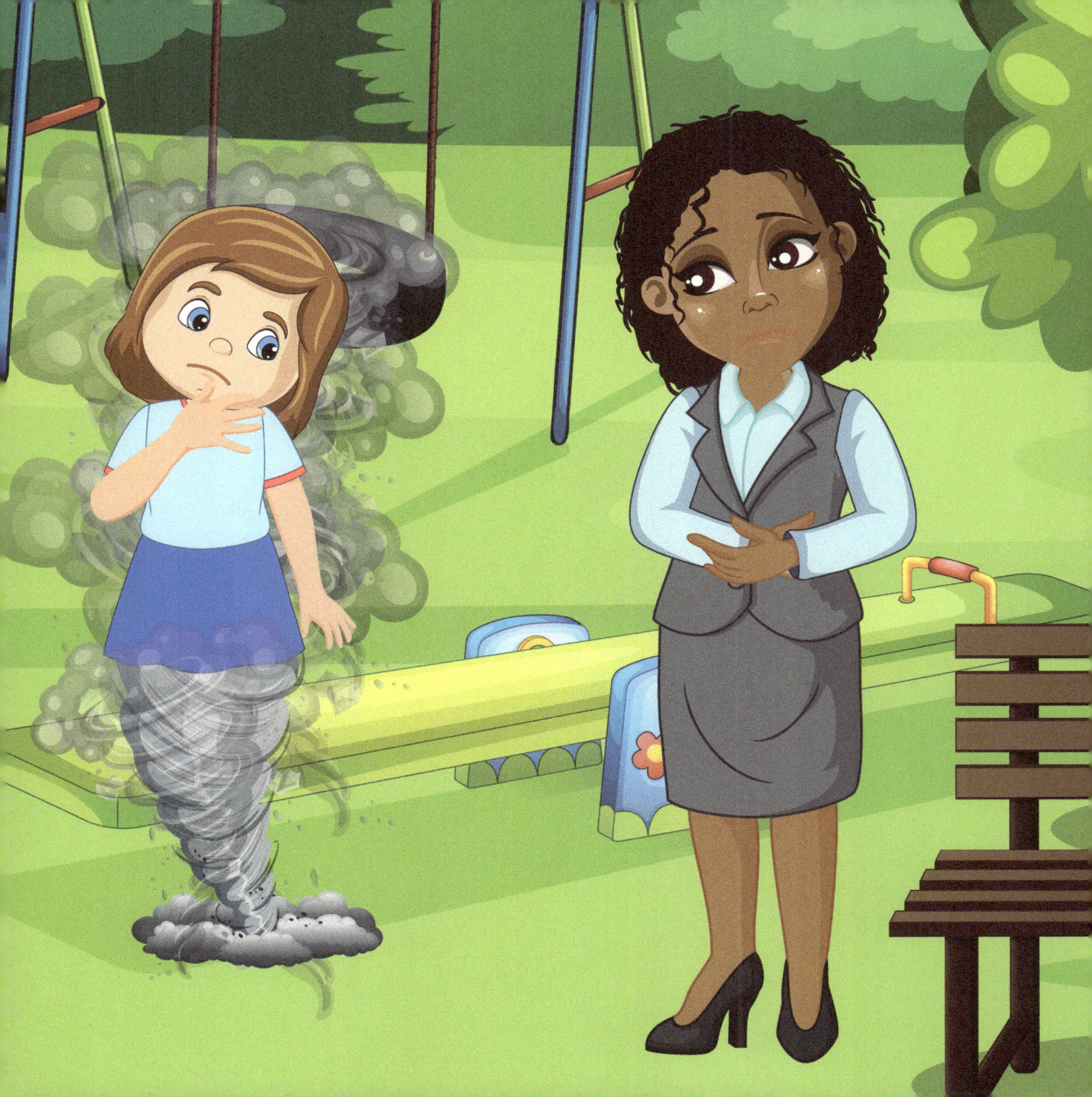

"You are so very special, Annie.
Let your personality show.
Give them time. They will soon see,
You're the best person they could know."

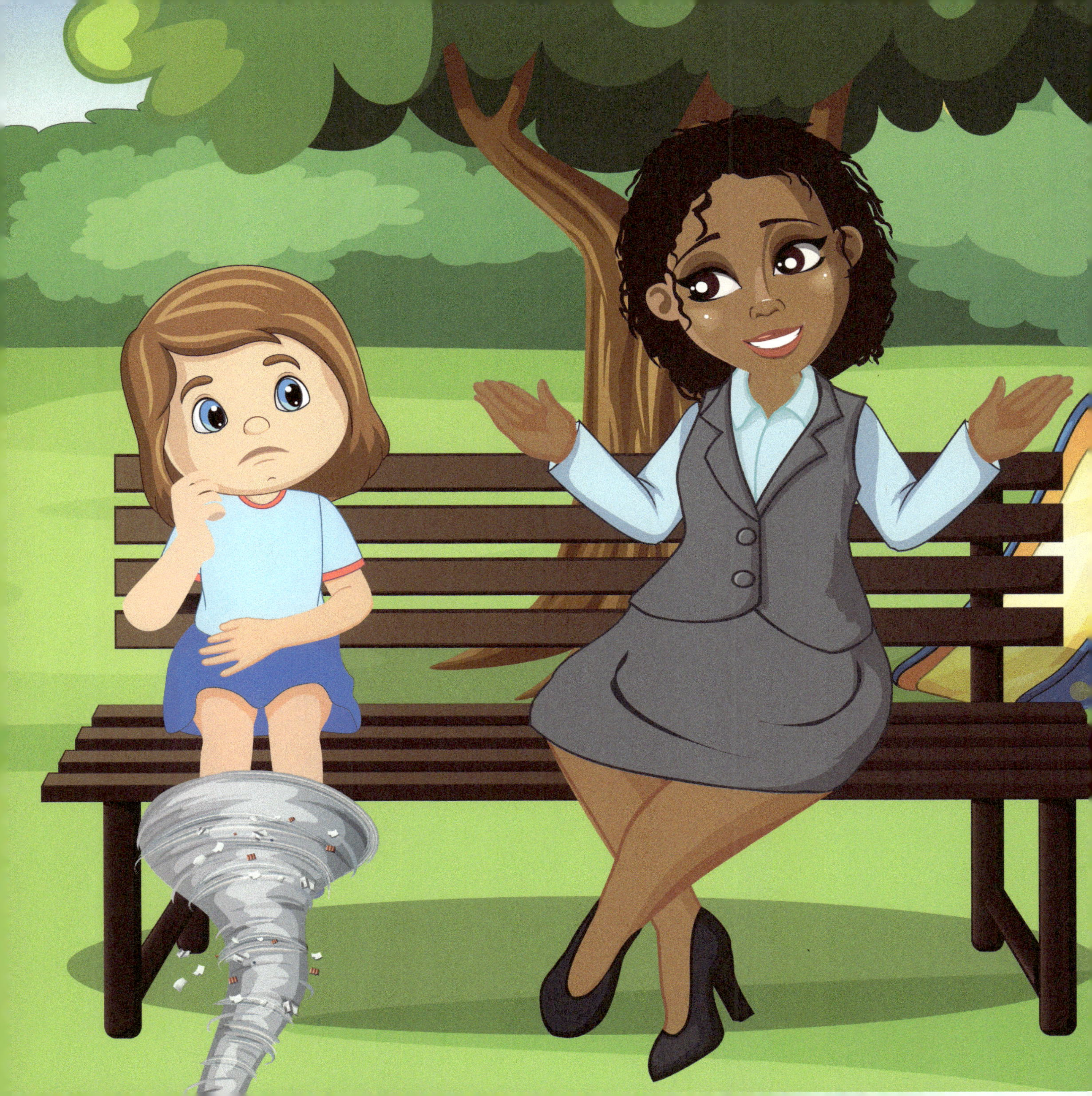

"Wow, Cyclone Annie!
Your cyclone is so cool.
It goes on and on, it never ends.
I'm Jacob. I am new here at the school."

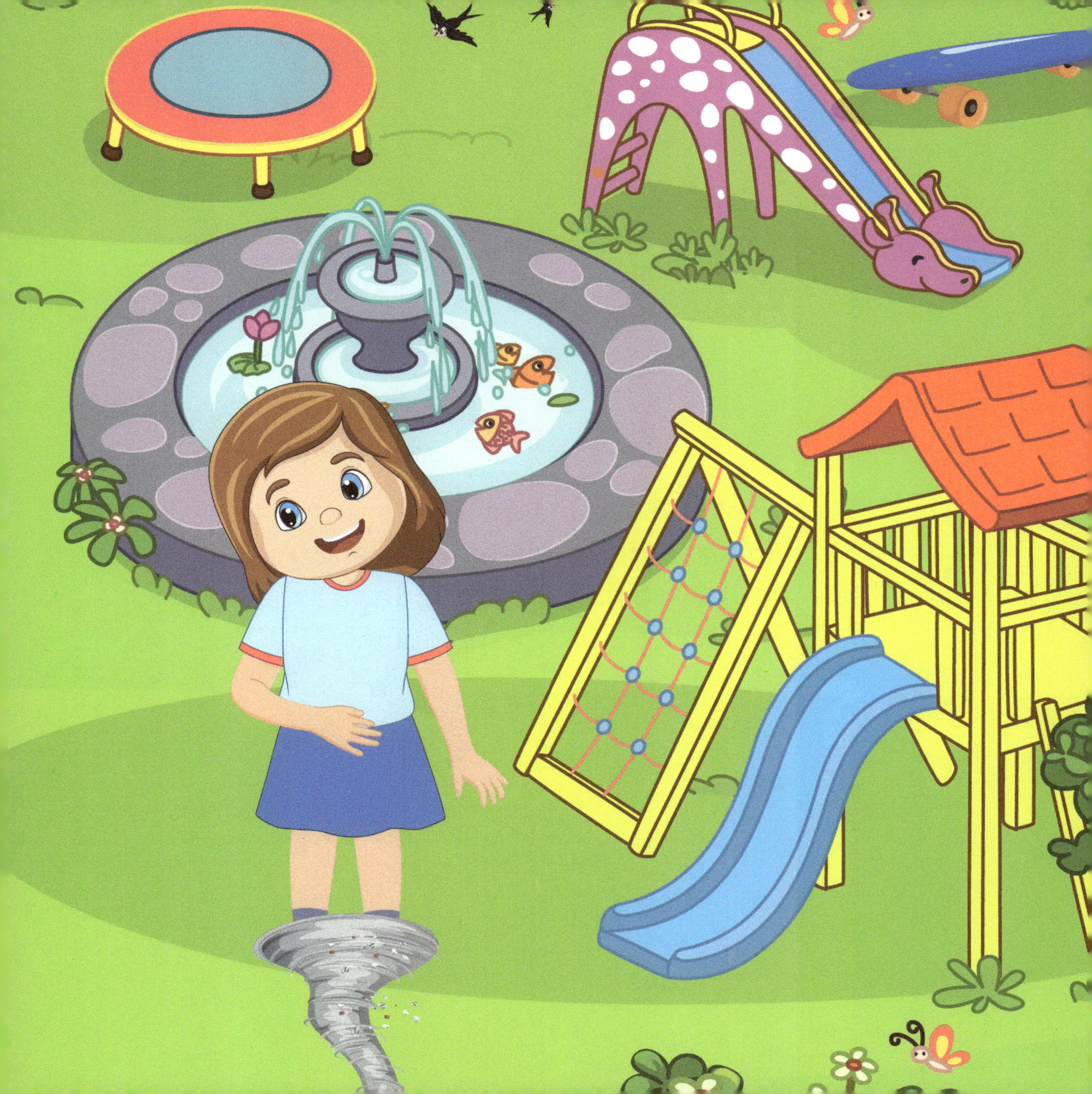

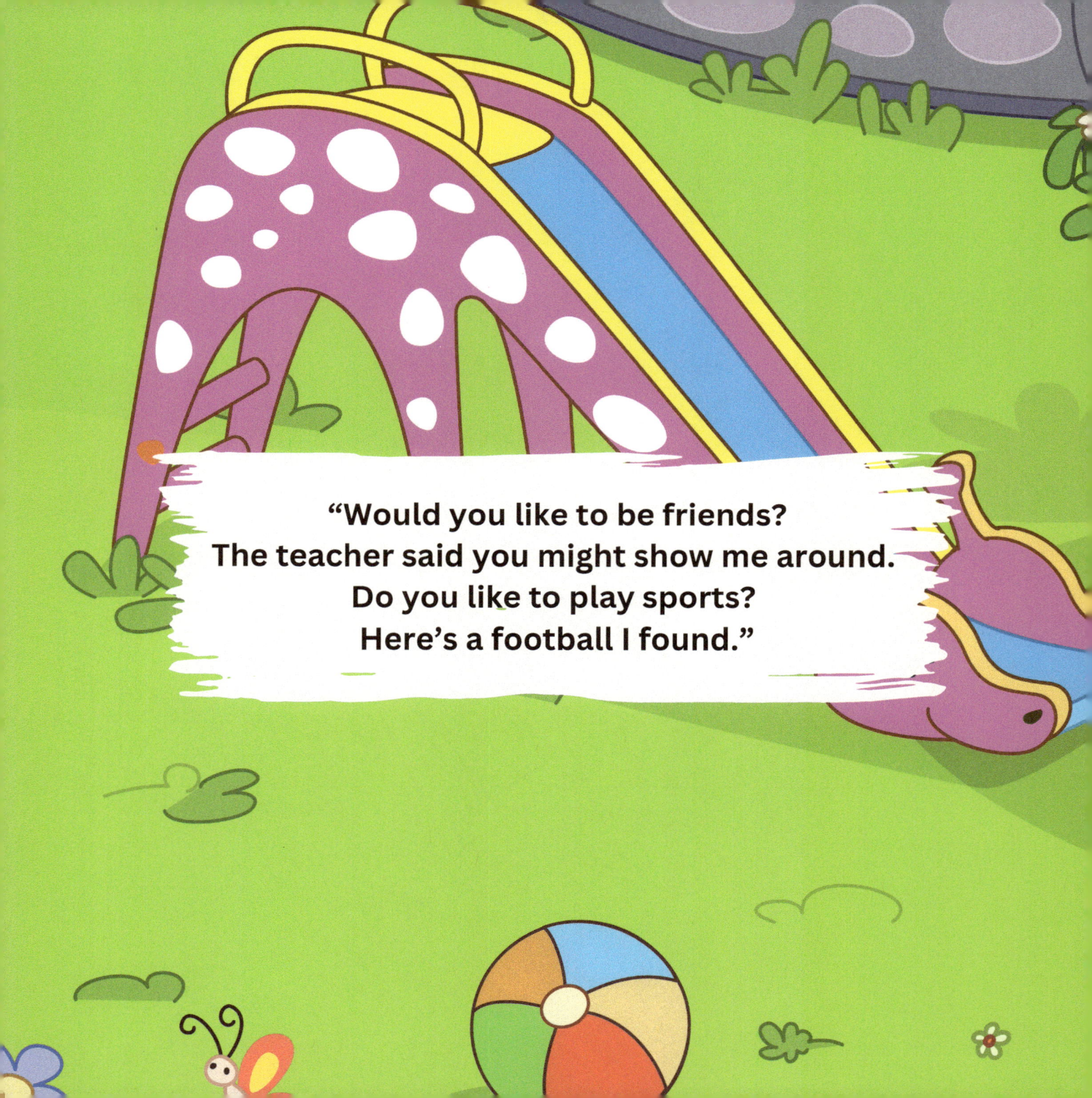

"Would you like to be friends?
The teacher said you might show me around.
Do you like to play sports?
Here's a football I found."

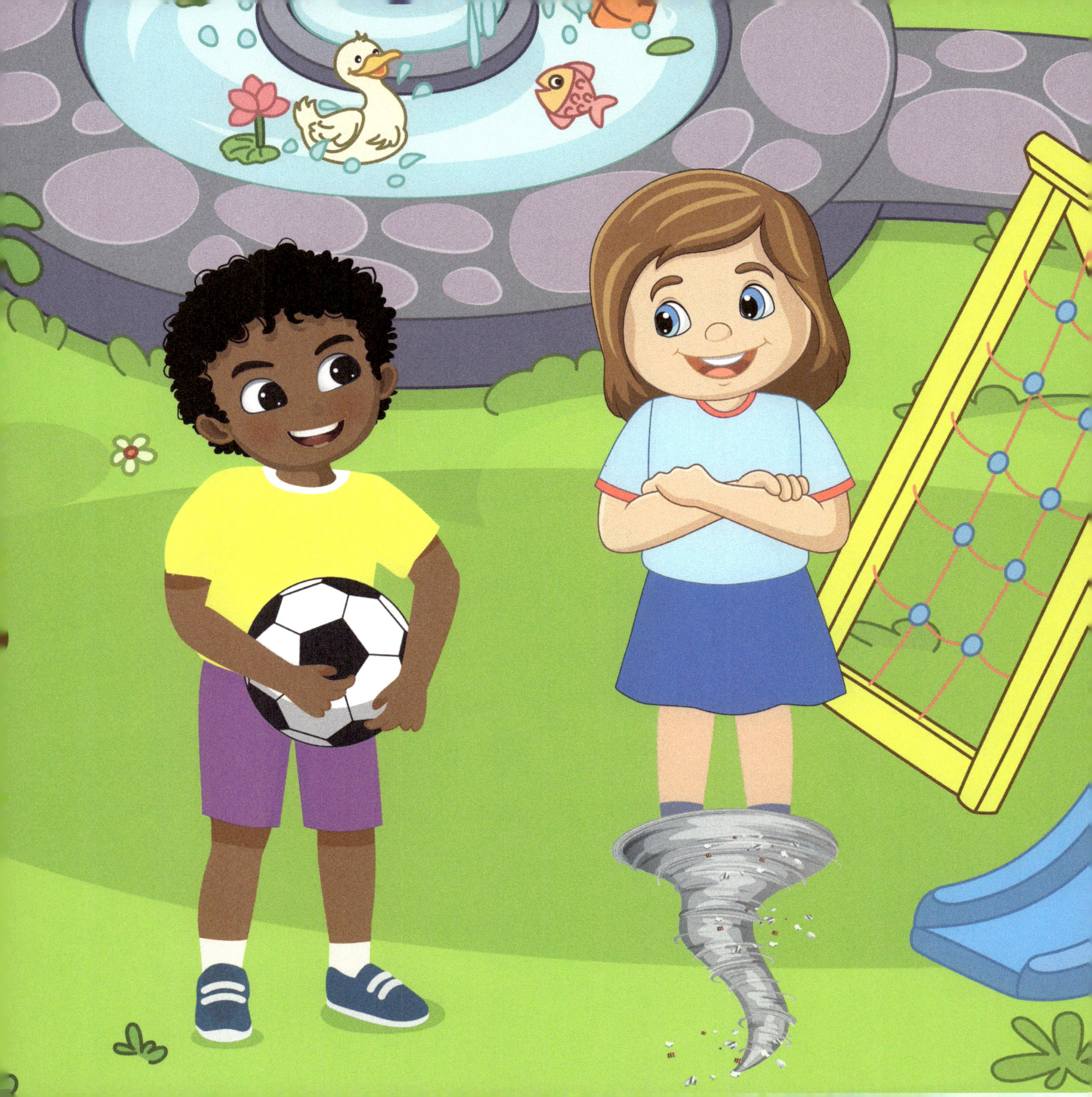

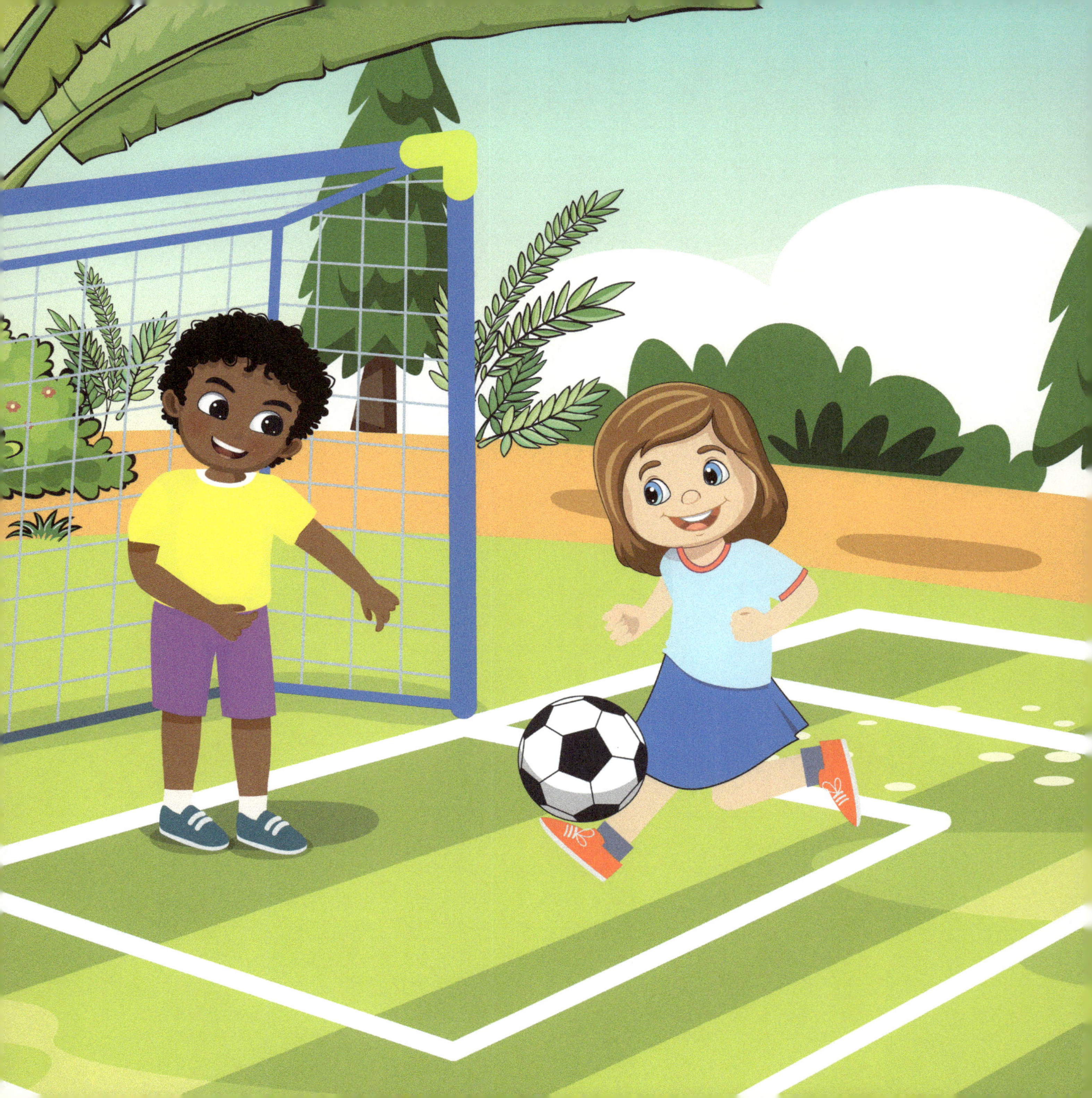

Annie's wind disappeared,
As they ran to the football field.
She laughed, played, ran and scored,
The fastest on the field.

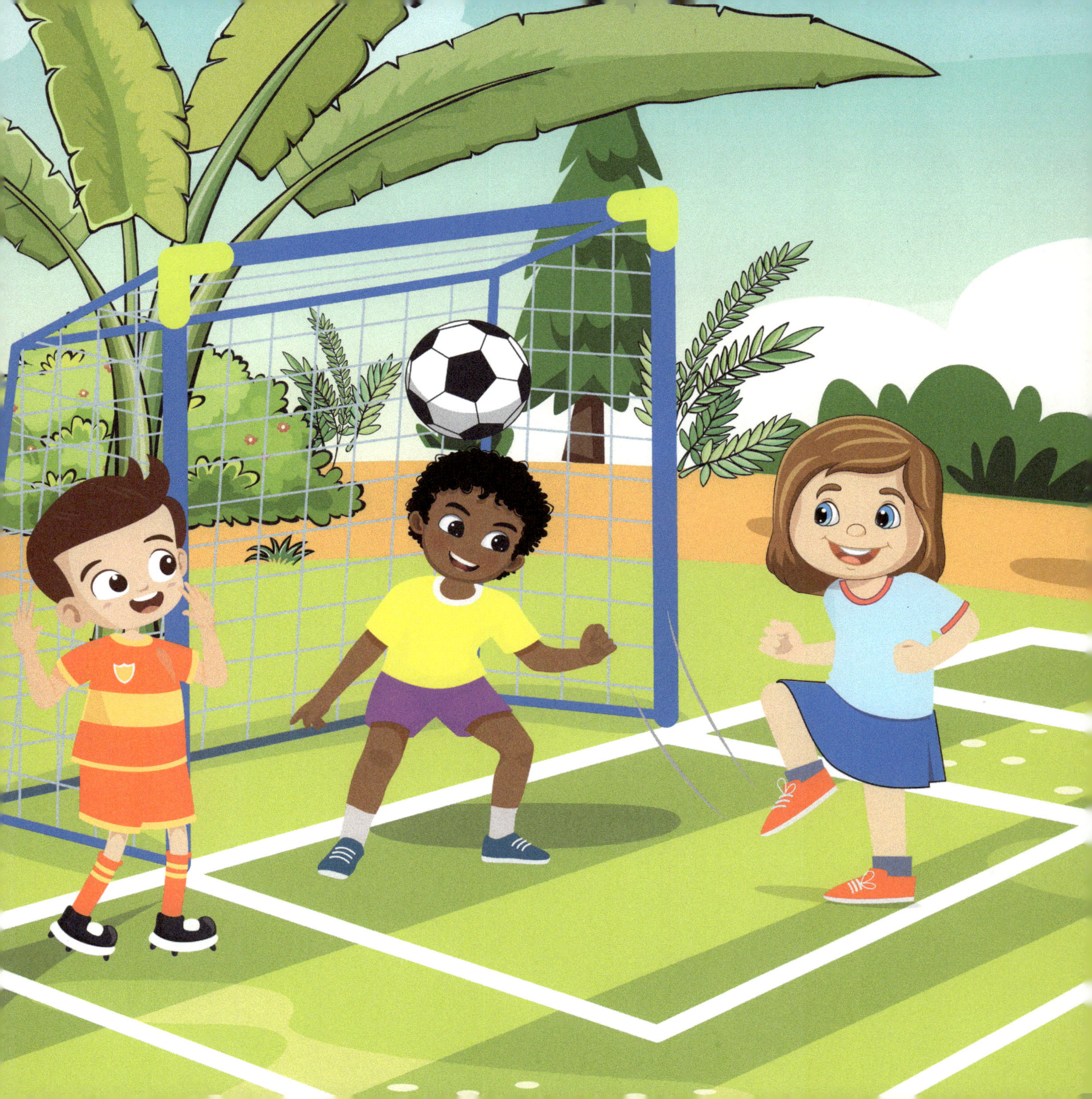

The other kids came out to look.
"Hey! She is really good!
Cyclone Annie, we are sorry.
We never understood."

Other titles by the author

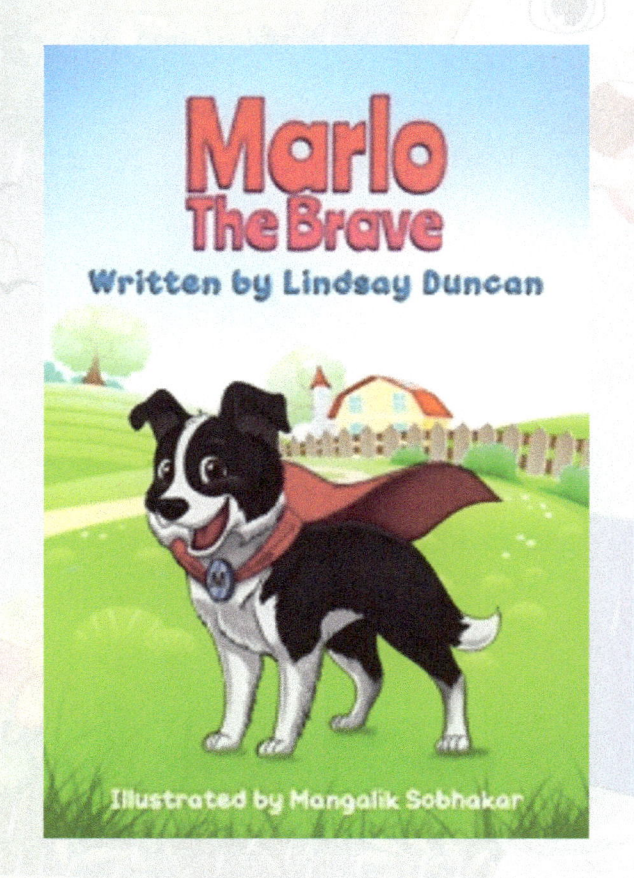

Interactive book.

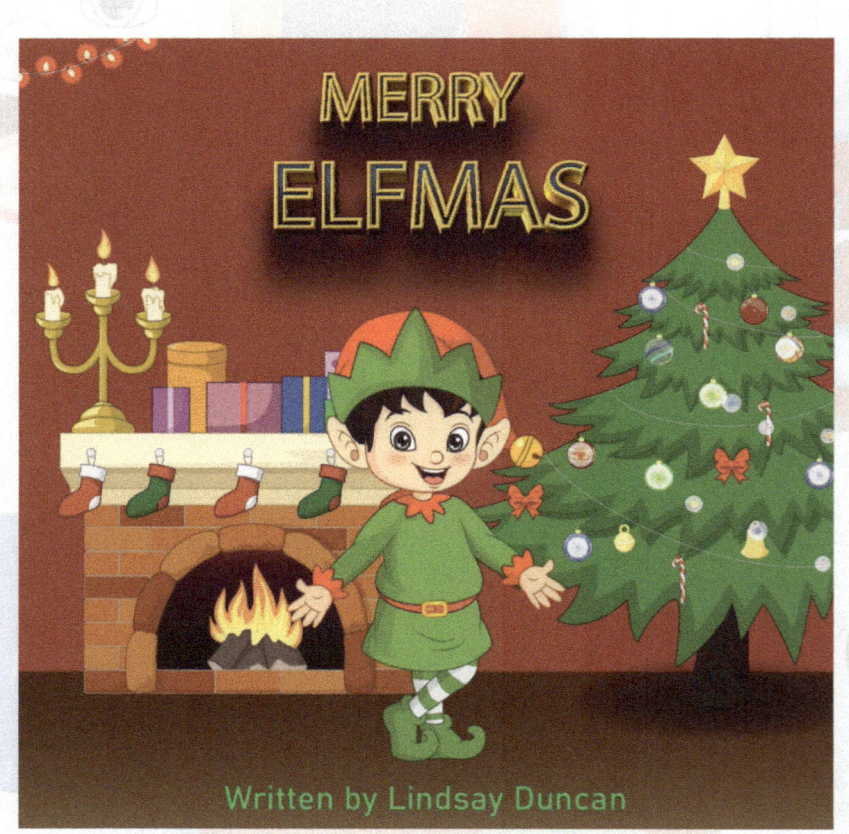

Rhyming book.

Milton Keynes UK
Ingram Content Group UK Ltd.
UKHW050949190224
438087UK00004B/18